GIZMO

Goes on the Christmas Express

eBook Designed by

SCHOLASTIC PUBLISHERS

Dedication

This book is dedicated to those on the Nice List.
You make the world better.

Gizmo loves snowflakes. He especially loves making snowflakes. One roll of tissue paper can decorate our entire house.

It was the night before Christmas,
and tucked deep in his bed,
Gizmo was waiting for sugar plums,
to dance in his head.

He wiggled and he squiggled,
but he couldn't fall asleep.
Nothing made him drowsy,
not even counting sheep.

He stared at the invitation,
engraved with his name.
One golden ticket to ride,
the Christmas Express Train.

It was good for one night only,
the night of Christmas Eve.
It smelled like milk and cookies,
and the stamp just said Believe.

The instructions were easy,
just drift off to dream.
The conductor will wake you,
with a whistle of steam.

As Gizmo began to doze,
the whistle startled him awake.
Blinding lights filled his room,
and the floor began to shake.

The Christmas Express was in his yard,
and half way down the road.
She was red, black and shiny,
and dusted with Christmas snow.

The conductor hung on to the train,
while yelling "ALL ABOARD".
His eyes glistened through the steam.
He could not be ignored.

All Aboard!

Gizmo climbed up the stairs,
and found a window seat.
Everyone was still in pajamas,
but tonight was not for sleep.

The conductor stood up at the front,
and loudly cleared his throat.
He rubbed his beard, squinted his eyes,
and smiled before he spoke.

"Welcome aboard the Christmas Express,
please kindly take your seat.
An entire year of being good,
has earned you this very special treat."

The whistle blew loud twice more,
as the train began to move.
The rails clanked, the wheels turned,
the engine went choo choo −choo choo.

Welcome Aboard the Christmas Express...

"Next stop we will be up north,
where magic fills the sky.
The snow sparkles like diamonds,
and reindeer really fly."

Then from the kitchen,
a dancing chef appeared.
He was handing out cookies,
grinning from ear to ear.

Someone from another car,
came skipping down the aisle,
singing "Who wants hot chocolate?"
and pouring it with a smile.

Gizmo ate his cookie.
He danced and sang along.
Then someone from the back yelled "STOP".
Oh oh....What could be wrong?

Gizmo couldn't believe his eyes.
It was that horrid elf.
The one always watching,
spying from a shelf.

The elf held up a picture,
and declared it evidence!
"Gizmo is a thief, he snarled,
he has no self defense."

Gizmo was blindsided,
the picture was definitely him,
but it wasn't what it looked like.
Things were looking grim.

The conductor looked at the photo.
"Oh my this is bad.
I'm so Sorry Gizmo,
but I'll need your ticket back."

Gizmo was so humiliated,
he didn't know what to do.
When the conductor took his ticket,
he didn't even try to argue.

He just stared out the window,
the North Pole was now in sight.
Maybe he could talk to Santa,
and try to make things right.

The train came to a grinding halt,
in front of Santa's Village.
Everyone was about to enjoy
their golden ticket privilege.

Gizmo was asked to stay on board,
while the others got to play.
They got to feed the reindeer.
They got to ride the sleigh.

Gizmo couldn't hold back the tears.
He had to clear his name.
He had to find Santa.
He had to explain.

Just then the door flew open,
a rush of cold air filled the space.
He heard a HO! HO! HO!,
and then he saw his face.

His eyes they did twinkle,
and his smile was oh so merry.
His beard was white as snow,
his nose, as red as a cherry.

He was dressed in red fur
with a fluffy, furry trim.
He looked just like the stories,
It had to be him.

Ho! Ho! Ho!

Santa looked at Gizmo,
and wiped away a tear.
"No more need for crying,
your name is in the clear.

I hope you will forgive,
my over zealous elf.
He saw you stealing popcorn,
and couldn't help himself.

He filed a report,
and tried to make you Naughty.
He didn't have the whole story.
His evidence was spotty.

He has a terrible habit,
of just looking for the bad.
So that's all he ever finds.
it's really pretty sad.

If he would spend his time
looking for the good,
He would be so much happier,
as anybody would.

You find what you seek,
so YOU have to decide.
You can look for the Naughty,
or look for the Nice.

The elf was mistaken
when he called you a thief.
He didn't see the garland,
He only saw deceit."

The elf climbed on board,
in a very bad mood.
He was still horrid and smug,
and noticeably rude.

"Don't worry about him.
He is not your concern.
The truth always prevails.
It's a lesson he'll learn.

You can't control
what others say or do.
But how you react,
that's 100% entirely up to you.

So always do what's right,
even when no one else can see.
And keep stringing that popcorn,
it looks great on the tree!"

The next thing Gizmo remembers,
is being back in his bed,
while visions of sugar plums
danced in his head.

Merry Christmas

Illustrated By River Wilson

River was 14 when we took the actual train ride in Palestine, Texas. Also pictured in the story is Brandy, River's beautiful mom... also Gizmo's sister.

Written By Heidi Heisel

Heidi is Gizmo mom. They travel together on many Adventures. The Gizmo Goes books tell the tales from Gizmos point of view.

Printed in the USA
CPSIA information can be obtained
at www.ICGtesting.com
LVHW071502091224
798688LV00015B/277